STORY QUILTS

APPALACHIAN WOMEN SPEAK

SHANNON HITCHCOCK &
ILLUSTRATIONS BY SOPHIE PAGE

History has forgotten most Appalachian women.
Many of them couldn't read or write.

They stayed close to home
and raised large families.

Appalachian women worked their fingers to the bone.

Cooking, cleaning, gardening, canning.

Then, at day's end, they threaded their needles,
reached for their rag bags,
pieced colorful squares,

and turned scraps into quilts that told stories.

Most every night, a girl would watch her Mama
sew by the kerosene lamp
until finally, she was old enough
to make quilt squares of her own.

She would reach into the rag bag and pull out scraps, maybe from an old apron. An apron faded so blue, it almost looked purple when the light hit it just right. An apron that had belonged to her granny.

The color reminded her of The Blue Ridge Mountains.

The mountains she called home.

She would sew those scraps together, stitch by stitch, hum a lonesome tune, maybe a ballad called "Fair Ellender," and remember when her granny sang that song to her.

That apron would be the heart of her quilt.

that kissed the mountains
and the snow that covered
them in winter.

She would piece together strips of yellow, orange, and pink.

merging the colors into blocks,
that blended like a mountain sunrise.

She would search for scraps the colors of mountain flowers.
Trillium, lady's slippers, columbines,
goldenrod, asters, and black-eyed Susans.

She might cut strips of muslin for a border,
long and rectangular.

Its evergreen hue reminding her of the pine trees
that stand tall among barren maples in the dead of winter.

She would move her quilt squares like puzzle pieces, until they told a story.

A story about the beauty of her mountains.
Then stitch them together, seam by seam.

History books don't say much
about Appalachian women.
Many of them couldn't read or write,
but they left behind patchwork quilts.
Some even hang on museum walls.

Quilts that whisper long
forgotten stories—

If you know how to listen.

AUTHOR'S NOTE

I got the idea for this book from an exhibit at the North Carolina Museum of History called *Quilt Speak—Uncovering Women's Voices Through Quilts.* It reminded me of my mother and my grandmother. Both pieced quilts that warmed our beds at night.

Educational opportunities were limited for women who grew up in remote, rural areas. Transportation was scarce, farm chores came before bookwork, and often winter weather kept children from attending school on a regular basis. Yet these women, who lacked formal education and money for supplies, still found ways to express themselves using only scraps, a needle, and thread.

Patchwork quilts remind us these women were thrifty. They didn't waste materials, even using old feed sacks. Their straight stitches and quilting patterns demonstrate these women took great pride in making quilts that not only kept their families warm but added beauty to their homes.

Quilting offered a chance to sing and tell family stories. It provided a creative outlet after a hard day's work. Women used this quiet time to pass down family traditions to their daughters. Sometimes girls made a game out of remembering which piece of old clothing the scraps came from.

History has forgotten most Appalachian women. Their voices were silenced by poverty, a lack of education, and society's expectation that a woman's place was in the home. It's only by seeking new ways of interpreting the past that their voices are heard.

Quilting is not as widespread as it used to be due to the ease of purchasing inexpensive blankets and quilts. To preserve quilting as an art form, the National Quilting Museum in Paducah Kentucky offers Quilt Camps, scout activities, a national School Block Challenge, and a Junior Quilters' Club. For more information or to join the School Block Challenge, visit www.quiltmuseum.org.

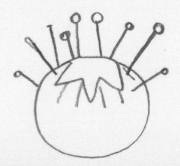

ILLUSTRATOR'S NOTE

While making the art for this book, I was inspired by so many beautiful and fascinating quilts. Here is a brief list of Southern women quilters whose work I found especially noteworthy:

- Elizabeth Graham Jacobs, 1909–2000. Columbus County, NC
- Eliza Helen Rogers Arrington, 1906–1984. Wake County, NC
- Emily Margaret Eller Maxwell, 1867–1957. Watauga County, NC
- Harriet Powers, 1837–1910. Clarke County, GA
- Kate Clayton "Granny" Donaldson, 1864–1960. Cherokee County, NC

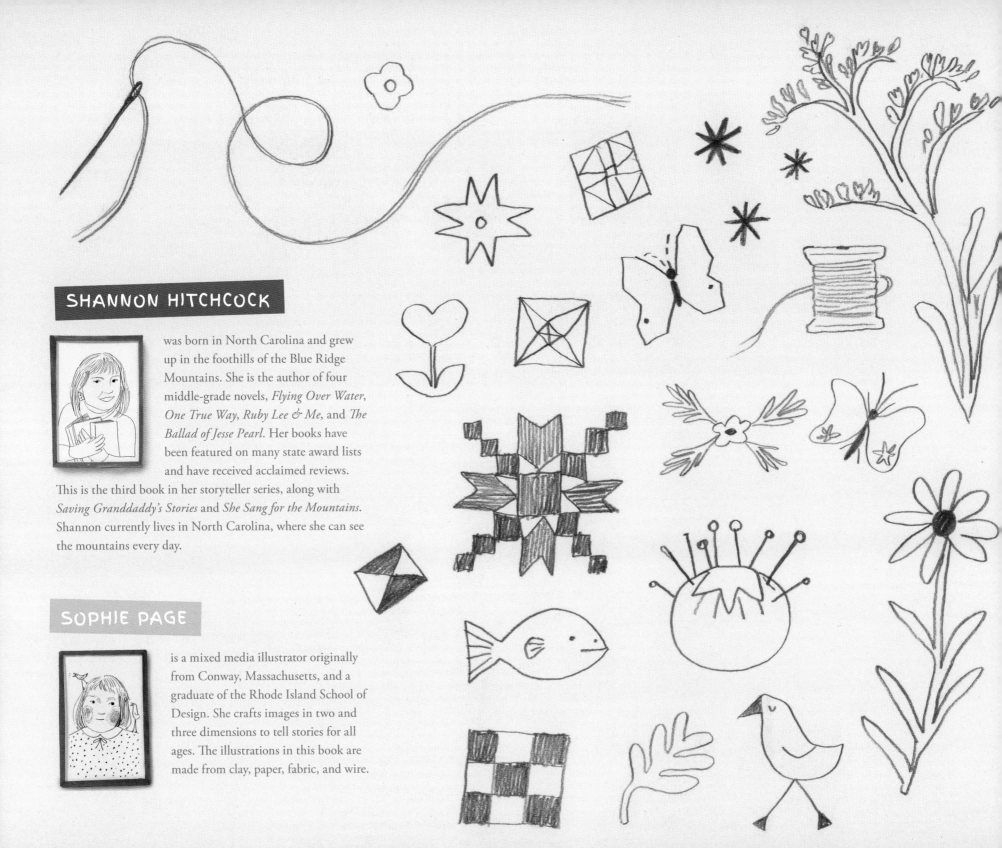

SHANNON HITCHCOCK

was born in North Carolina and grew up in the foothills of the Blue Ridge Mountains. She is the author of four middle-grade novels, *Flying Over Water*, *One True Way*, *Ruby Lee & Me*, and *The Ballad of Jesse Pearl*. Her books have been featured on many state award lists and have received acclaimed reviews. This is the third book in her storyteller series, along with *Saving Granddaddy's Stories* and *She Sang for the Mountains*. Shannon currently lives in North Carolina, where she can see the mountains every day.

SOPHIE PAGE

is a mixed media illustrator originally from Conway, Massachusetts, and a graduate of the Rhode Island School of Design. She crafts images in two and three dimensions to tell stories for all ages. The illustrations in this book are made from clay, paper, fabric, and wire.